LEAVE HER WILD

Samantha Lazo

For women and the girls they once were.

For my Zuri and the other wild ones.

CONTENTS

FORWARD

I didn't want to write this.

I was called to write it by the girl within me that I was pushed to face once my daughter came into this world.

She awakened me to a voice that had been dormant most of my life. These poems are that voice. They unpack how the world tames our minds and bodies as girls so we never fully see and sink into our souls as women.

These poems. This voice. They are here to set it all on fire for young girls, so the world will love them, but leave them wild.

MIND

Before I could comprehend sounds, letters, words
before I could count by ones, twos, threes
I was being filled with stories about hes and shes.
Before I could point to my mouth, belly, chest
before I could say my own name
I was being flooded with body shame.
Before I could sit, crawl, stand
smile, laugh, hold hands
there was a world of demand
already waiting for me.

— it starts before we are born

The narratives we are fed
the ones we swallow
give the illusion we are full
that everything we need
will be served to us in handfuls.
Later, we wake to a table
with no place setting
in its place: systems abetting
our womanhood
our truth
our stories
with ones that paint us
emotional, irrational, malicious.
And despite our energy
being the most nutritious
part of everyone's meal
of every feed
every bite
every need
they'll tell us to be grateful.
Sit down.
Eat.

A conversation between a grown man and my nephew:

"What is your favorite color?"

Sparkly blue, I also like pink.

"Those are for girls, why not a nice hunter green?"

It's subtle
sneaky
easy
to ignore.
Such complicity
puts them into boxes
with no air.
How unfair
to destroy his joy
make him think less of pink
or that if a boy likes sparkles he'll shrink.
These tall tales
are the beginning of how we fail.

Emotions in cuffs
breasts, belly, and brain behind bars—
on constant patrol to control
how I dressed
I socialized
even how I cried.
What I saw on screens
in magazines
did not match this policing.
It all had me confused
What was I supposed to be?
To do?

      — policing girlhood

"Peter Peter Pumpkin eater,
Had a wife but couldn't keep her;
He put her in a pumpkin shell
And there he kept her very well."

In other words...

Men can keep you even if
you do not want to be kept
men being forceful is normal
something we must accept.

"There was an old woman who lived in a shoe
She had so many children she did not know what to do;
She gave them some broth without any bread;
She whipped them all soundly and put them to bed."

In other words...

Being a lone woman is shameful.
Women are primary caretakers
even when it's painful.
A father can disappear without consequence
when he does, a mother isn't allowed
to get emotional over his incompetence.

"What are little boys made of?
What are little boys made of?
Snips and snails,
And puppy-dog tails.
That's what little boys are made of!

What are little girls made of?
What are little girls made of?
Sugar and spice,
And everything nice."

In other words...

Boys can be dirty, playful, gross,
but girls must be prim, proper, nice.
Girls must be graceful
while boys can be distasteful.
A boy's poor behavior
will be written off as normal
while a girl's will be seen as mournful.

I fear I've forgotten how to frown or seethe.
My expression fixed to avoid any regression you may inflict
so here are the whites of my teeth.
Mouth pinned into peaks at my cheeks
because that's what girls are supposed to do:

                                                      smile.

"Watch your smart mouth little girl."
Don't show them your brilliance
they haven't enough resilience
to handle that they cannot teach you something new.
You must act surprised, grateful, tasteful.
Correcting and resetting
will activate their fragility
and then, well,
they will treat you differently.

My mind was so full of toxic narratives,
I could hardly call it mine.

"Stay humble."

— another lesson in keeping us small

Most nights we would watch my mother fall asleep on the couch, waiting for my father to come home. She never knew what hour that might be— just sitting in wait, alone in the unknown. When he arrived, he would float right by her, put orange push-up pops in our tiny hands, tell us how much he loved us, and go eat the dinner my mother prepared hours before. The dinner we had already eaten without him.

— lessons in a woman's role

Maybe I am too forward
Good girls don't make the first move
he must feel he's won, willed, worked for it
or else you will not have been worth it.

Maybe I am too vocal
Good girls don't speak up, they sit back, play their role
roll with it, submit to his control, so he feels like a man.

Maybe I am too emotional
Good girls don't have emotions unless they are the ones
he can fix, console, make whole so he feels valuable.

Maybe I am too _____
I guess I'll always be too this, too that
too something for some reason
I am not meant to understand
so I'll stand here.
Just stand here
and be nothing.

I watched how men treated the women in my life
their body language, their words a knife
rife with unwanted direction, insulting advice.
They'd cut her talk
chop the top of her words off
explain things she already knew the answer to.
A strange exchange.
They never stopped the hims
never forced their blade away.
A picture of fear
seared and framed
in my brain.

"Men like women that can cook and clean."

— how domestication begins

We move quietly in every space
our noises discrete
light on our feet.

We speak calmly in every air
our pitch just right
soft, polite.

We cross our legs
hands on our laps
take up less space
allowing you to fill the gaps.

        — palatability training

I learned what a woman was from men.
Me and every woman before me
manufactured for their comfort
lost in their loudness.
Our actual womanhood silenced
so their power could pulse, pressure, grow.
Grow so loud it would cloud our space
make us quiet
make us quaint.

Have you ever wondered
why storms are sometimes sudden?
Mother Nature knows our strength
and she winces every time we say "sorry"

Women are wild, alluring, fierce.
Many will fail to see what fuels such a trinity:
love, softness, peace.

— the unnoticed layers

Hold space for everyone's emotions
you are responsible for how they feel.
Make sure you conceal your own
otherwise, they will see you as wild, not wise.
Exercise restraint from relating or comparing
someone who is selfless and caring
does not participate in oversharing.
Hold space for everyone's emotions
tend to them because that is your maternal duty
your instinct, it will keep you loved, keep you linked.
So I sit here with no space left
not a corner, cubby, or shelf for myself.

A woman's wit is endearing
because it dares to make you soft.
It challenges your intelligence
and you love it, it turns you on.
You fawn over our sarcasm
you savor it when we throw our sass around
but why then, in the next breath
you don't want us to make a sound?

For those that praise women and girls for being bold but become bitter when it bites, you don't truly love her boldness, you only love when it enables you because the minute it disables you from always being right

your love takes flight.

Some are not worthy of language
the raw divinity entangled in it
because they use it for anguish
an attempt to vanquish
our warmth
our wealth
our worth

    — language weaponized against women

I wonder where they go
the words women swallow
the words they hold back
out of fear of attack.
Maybe that's why
our faces are easy to read
all those words sink into
our skin, they feed
on our patience
our grace.

Loving ourselves as women is a pill laced with guilt and shame because when we claim that we contain magnitudes we are greeted with

"how conceited"   "she's stuck up"

         "how vain"
                        "okay, that's enough"

So we swallow the idea that we are shallow and allow the guilt and shame to numb the pain that comes with keeping our confidence concealed.

I thought it was me
that I was the one
always biting my tongue
my teeth
my jaw
my saw
cutting the words short.

>*I wielded the tools, so*
>*how could my silencing*
>*be caused by these fools?*

Ahh, I see.
I allowed their beliefs
to seep in heaps
so deep inside my worth
they atrophied
that muscle in my mouth
saturated my words with doubt.

There is an entire dictionary
hidden somewhere within me.
Between its covers:
words, phrases, pages upon pages
of things I wanted to say but wouldn't
things I should have said but couldn't.
I was taught that women are a utility
to protect male fragility
so I played my voice small
let every letter crawl
back down my throat
not a single sound left afloat.
My hope?
I'll throw it all up one day.
A language, a lesson
in the dangers of lessening.

A career
A man
A child
the end.

    — society's portrait of the fulfilled woman

Samantha
Age: 25
Gender: Female
Interested in: men
Location: wherever you are

Dating Profile Summary

I'm an ELA teacher that loves to read, write, listen to live music, and travel. I am outgoing, fun-loving, and enjoy spontaneous adventures to new restaurants, nature destinations, dive bars, and hidden gems where dessert is served. But I will change all of that if you decide you do not like it. What you need supersedes me. I am a good woman. I promise.

Your job is to make him feel powerful, dominant, invincible.

What they didn't tell me is how this need to feed their control would take a toll on me. I minimized my voice in service of them, erased my cares, my ideas, shifted gears because women are not meant to be providers or powerful, oh no, because if we were, oh if we were...

Women are groomed to be the best meal you've ever had, the most palatable imaginable. Polite, keeping it light on the taste buds, but not too faint, they demand depth, a richer taste. And when our bite has spice, a little bitter fight, they'll call for a more delicate element, a decadent display of passive play. You see, while women contain layers of flavors, courses upon courses of profound forces, we must be palatable to be at the table.

What a waste of taste.

Our brilliance must be calculated and just dull enough for it to feel pleasant, not rough. Polished, next to perfect, but not too perfect, that's a defect. Don't mess up, trip up, slip up, or your time will be cut short.

They joke "It must be that time of the month."
They don't even grant the courtesy of asking. No.
They declare it just as they declare, defame, and claim
everything. They mock the very mechanism that makes
their lives possible.

Their propensity to ridicule the intensity required to bring
them into this world made me think:

> They say things like this out of fear for what they
> do not understand, just constant ribbing and
> reprimand. They can keep their fear, their
> ill-informed insinuations, their inclination toward
> weakness.
>
> My mission is bigger than fear or petty
> commentary. My mission makes such vomit
> arbitrary. The next time someone barks "It must
> be that time of the month" it will be a mark of
> respect regarding my arrival.

I forever chose men over myself.
Fulfilling their needs to make me needed.
Serving their dreams to make me dreamy.
Satisfying their desires to make me desirable.
A narrative on repeat.
One that swallowed me entirely.
Who was I if I didn't fulfill, serve, satisfy?
Who even was I without them?

Being a woman is a wonder, isn't it?
Be everything and nothing at the same time.
Have a voice, but make sure it's quiet
reserved, coy, *don't start a riot*.
Understand my emotions, but don't show your own
no crying, no feeling, *watch your tone*.
Share your opinions, but make sure they're like mine
safe, subtle, *get in line*.
Love your body, but don't show it to others
reserved, decent, *aren't you someone's mother?*

Yeah. Being a woman is a wonder
and you wonder why we're
screaming
seething
sour.

They were taught just as much as we were.
suppress the tenderness
an internal mess
masculine
manly
macho
The world does not want to see
a man's emotions, his glee.
Bury it before it can touch you
or me.
Bury it for no one to see.
Leaving us with a man
once soft as sand
now hardened
hollow
hiding.

What if?
What if I let them run
in the spaces fragile men control?
I imagine discomfort
would sizzle up their spines
hijack their nerves
frenzy their fears.
They were not given
the lessons on lessening
the lectures on controlled gestures.
What a gorgeous mess I'd make
if I let my emotions
flow like oceans
in such spaces.

We hide our tears in fear of the label: *emotional woman*
But when we let them flow
they humanize the world
cleanse it
soften its hardened heart.
So why conceal them
when their release could cease
the way the world locks up pain?

our emotions make them emotional

— irony

We say it without thinking because it is deeply rooted in our shrinking. It implies we don't have the right to say or do what we want, and after it rolls off our tongues it haunts. Its submissiveness eats our consciousness. Our internalized doubt never sees its way out, so we coat every statement in apology, "I'm sorry" "I'm sorry" "I'm sorry" even though we are not.

I wonder what would grow
if women planted every "sorry"
that rolled off their tongues.
A garden of wildflowers so vast
its scent would coat your lungs?
A forest of oaks so strong
its branches would reach the sun?
A field of fruit so broad
without it we couldn't feed the young?

The narratives cut my heart open
looked me in the eye
and told me I wasn't allowed to bleed.

I found an old photo of myself
wedged between some notebook pages
that carried love letters and longing for someone else.
I barely recognized her.
Side-swiped bangs, sheepish smile
shoulders slightly curled as if to say
"I am sorry. I am not sure I belong here."
Hands awkwardly folded in front of a silk button-up
likely from the dollar store as if to say
"I am sorry. My body is weird."
Drenched in innocence
foreign to confidence.
A product of the bullshit
she'd been fed.
But still, she glowed.
I guess the glow
was always there.
She just needed to leave
the tall tales behind
to rise from her chair.

BODY

This body has never felt like mine.
So many spaces I place it in
consume it with
unwelcomed eyes
ill intentions disguised.
This body has never felt like mine.

I used to lay down
splayed across beds
skin bare
vulnerability occupying the air
thinking men meeting my eyes
on the other side
would share in it
see my body as a sunrise
but they stayed guarded
stayed tough
stayed manly
"Why can't he?"
"Am I not enough?"

— toxic masculinity, the enemy of sexual encounters

"too…"

— the most harmful word to a woman's body

"Oh darling, boys will be boys."
"They are mischievous by nature, not as mature."
A sentiment that dismissed danger.

So I shared my toys with such boys
without thought or question
because when they took them without asking
they faced no consequence
they were the exception.

And when I was becoming a woman
this narrative grew and grew.
They saw new toys they felt entitled to.
Only they were not toys
they were fastened to this body
living limbs affixed to my skin
but hey "boys will be boys"
they don't understand
besides, your "no" sounded bland
it lacked surety, demand.

So I was responsible for their actions, reactions
and I internalized that my body was made
for such transactions.

Boys will be boys as long as we allow it.
But oh, just imagine if we showed them
made them see
what beautiful humans they can truly be.
Cease the repetition
let their radiance come to fruition.
No more "boys will be boys"
instead "boys will be poised"

There's a breed of compliment out there that is always transactional. A simple thank you is never enough. You have to empty your wallet with uncomfortable small talk and maybe a walk where they are not invited but your "thank you" had them excited and thinking they were entitled to more of you. It's as if they expect supplement for a compliment, and if we don't complete the transaction, they take action because to them a debt is owed. And if we default, they get their bag using verbal assault: "ungrateful bitch" "you aren't even that pretty anyway"

So what are we women to do with these transactional compliments we refuse to pay for?

I guess, we are just meant to endure.

It is a foreign word to them because for centuries women have hid it under their tongues, in the backs of their throats, in the hollow spaces behind their hearts.

It is a foreign word to them because this world has created entitled men.

It is a foreign word to them because they believe your body is payment for "allowing" such an arrangement.

It is foreign to them, they'll pretend you don't mean it, deem it you playing "hard to get."

Two letters they refuse to comprehend, and when we say them they amend, bend, twist our intention to fit their story.

    — when women say "no"

If the tenderness you show me when my bare body meets your eyes disappears tomorrow when my legs, my shoulders, my thighs are covered upon sunrise, then it was never tenderness at all. Simply a scheme to get past my walls.
And that is okay.
I feel sorry for you
moving through life so
empty
vacant
untrue.

Faith fled this temple
before I knew what
it was capable of.
Before I knew it could
harness the stars
to bring life into the world.
Prayer turned to despair
with every standard
this body couldn't meet.
And it wasn't a doctor
or a man that cured it.
No.
It was motherhood
that restored my worship.

Boobs
Ta Tas
Titties
All terms in an attempt to sexualize what we are born with,
to sexualize a life source, magic, sustenance.

More attractive than any thigh gap
any filter, fitted dress, flirty skirt
any thong, lace, or breast-hugging shirt
any scrub, serum, soap
any sway, speech, or jewels around your throat.

    — self-awareness and self-love

When it comes to us
we want only two things:
to love and own our bodies.
Some make that feel impossible.

I wish your words weren't so sticky
slandering the radiant empire
that is a woman's body.
Covering her light
with words that fight
make her second guess
make her feel like less.
Yes.
I wish your words
weren't so sticky.

Every turn of a page
every click of a remote
every casual scroll
we are being told
our bodies do not carry
the sweetness of berries
the rune of rain songs.
No, all these images
erase our natural beauty
gone.
We are expected to rise
ascribe
to a different portrait
painted with traits unlike
what we are born with.

Man: "That's not what a real woman looks like"

Me: "Is she not a real woman?"

Man: "You know what I mean, she is all plastic."

Me: "The definition of the word real is something that exists in fact or in our physical world. So plastic surgery makes her 'not real'? Because she has plastic surgery she no longer exists?"

Man: "You know what I mean."

Me: "Clearly, I do not."

Real women don't get plastic surgery.
Real women don't use filters.
Real women don't need make-up.
Real women don't _____.

How about we just don't.
All. women.are.real.despite.how.you.feel.

Physically shrinking my body to fit beauty standards.
Another way the world teaches girls to be small.

The weekend comes.
Dance floors waiting.

The checklist:
- ☐ Freshly shaven legs + armpits + bikini area
  in case I meet a guy because why else would a
  woman shave?
- ☐ Make-up
  in case I meet a guy because why else would a
  woman wear make-up?
- ☐ Dope outfit
  in case I meet a guy because why else would a
  woman wear a dope outfit?

"In case I meet a guy..."
All I really wanted to do
was dance.
Alone.

Mirrors used to be my enemy. I would stare at myself for hours in search of every defect instead of honoring the beauty that stood before me. I'd pick out each flaw like petals off a flower. Pick and pick and pick until the stem stood solo, just the empty bones where beauty once blossomed.

The world loves to tell women when their time is up.
your wrinkles are deep
your body washed up
you're a mother now
sit down.

The thing about time, though
it is infinite.
And so are we.

Pictures are the worst. The pressure to press my body against someone else in order to memorialize a moment in time, while his hand climbs and climbs around the small of my back and dips lower and lower until I wince and shutter and the utter audacity that he thinks he can take liberties with my body for a fucking picture. I am not a fixture for you to fondle, nor am I a furnishing free for you to touch, but you will think nothing of it to dip your hands in my honey because society has taught you my body is yours and society has taught me to endure. So I stand there and hope they take the picture fast so this doesn't have to last...any longer.

It happens quickly. A gesture of "I am happy to see you" an embrace to say "It's been a while" plummets to hostile when you pull me closer than I'd like so my breasts rest on your chest or you grope my back in ways that make you feel full. I pull and pull and pull away. My backward pedal has you unsettled, so you shame me for your violation, your invasion of my body all because you felt owed access to it.

Younger me wished for everyone else's image
bigger breasts, wider hips
thinner waist, pouty lips.
I saw my body as a utility, reaching for perfection
to receive everyone else's affection but my own.

What I understand now?
Perfection is an ever-shifting illusion
an act of collusion that thrives on us
not believing we are born enough.

I would ask you to speak strictly with your eyes
because your words have damaged women before
but your gaze has also been known to graze
our bodies
to consume them without permission
make us uncomfortable
coax us into submission.
So I guess I'll just stand here
wishing to disappear.

Him: "What is your favorite feature about yourself?"

Me: "I am not sure."

Him: "Well, I love your legs, your lips, the way your hips are dipped in sugar."

Me: "Really? That's so sweet."

Words live within and on the skin.
The jabs that fall out of your mouth
sink into our minds
paint our cheeks, our shoulders, our thighs.

    — words can be violence

Your body is a temple.
What a beautiful sentiment.
Until you realize the deed to the temple
this "holy" place
is not in your hands
and it is rarely met with grace.

I found myself apologizing to men for my body.
Not in ways you might think. I never said, "I am sorry."
"I'm sorry I am so fat."
"I am sorry I am not as fit as the other women you've dated."
No, the apologizing came in agonizing choices
I've been conditioned to make for the sake of the male gaze.
I'd say I wasn't hungry to humbly avoid you seeing me eat.
I'd turn off the lights during sex to spare you having to bear
witness to my body's imperfections.
I'd buy every product possible to fix my flaws.
Your ears never heard me say "I'm sorry for my body."
But your eyes?
Your eyes did
loud and clear.

Our bodies break
to bring life into the world
and they rebuild
regenerate
recreate themselves
only for society
to cast its hammer upon us
"Why hasn't she bounced back?"
"She's a mother, why is she wearing that?"
"What a shame, she let herself go."
a never-ending hail of nails.

It's all done quite surgically
stitched into our hearts and minds
that because we have a portal between our thighs
this somehow makes us compromised
in need of men's protection
their strength, their direction.
Strange though isn't it?
The only people entering our portals
are such men who think themselves immortal.
So why when met with such pressure from one man
I am meant to reach for a different one's hand?
Why a man's protection is the fix
when a different one breaches the dips in my hips?
It all seems quite an ironic mess
that I should run from one reaching up my dress
into the arms of another.
But I digress.

We are not born hating our bodies.
The hate is calculated.
Perpetuated and exacerbated
by the need to keep us small.
It comes in manufactured phrases
throughout various phases
of our girlhood:

"Your midriff is indecent"
cue shame.

      "Her boobs are too big"
      cue shame.

        "You're too thin."
        cue shame.

          "Make-up will fix that"
          cue shame.

And shame remains.
Until we realize
all this was through your eyes
so we shut them
and open our own.

I'd overhear cafeteria commentary at school
boys discussing their checklists for girls.

"She's got to have a great ass."
"I want my girl to be athletic."
"A flat stomach and a nice smile."
"Bro, she can't be too skinny though".
"If she's a but-her-face, I can always fuck her from behind."

Nothing about her being a tender friend
An artist with a steady hand
A free spirit that'll dance without music
A rugged and loving soul that always gets through it

And sure, we girls did the same
we ooo'd and aww'd over the smile, the hair
the way they would stare with stars in their eyes.
But this wasn't the limit.
No, our words spanned the entire being
they glowed with empathy
they were powdered with love, not lust
because for us?
We wanted a mouth that raved
about us crushing the math test
we wanted a heart that remained
the same no matter who was around
we wanted a soul to connect with
not just a body to have sex with.
Our "checklist"
served connection.
It wasn't a collection
of notches for our belts
or a pool of insensitive verbal welts.

I was always racing to the end of: *pretty, prettier, prettiest*
As if being pretty was the goal, the greatest gain of my existence. But looking at my daughter has carved a vast distance between me and the notion that our worth lies in what everyone else sees. Watching her ponder, wonder, dance, and design solidifies that being pretty is the least interesting thing about us.

It will take the magic of the moon and the glow of the stars to make me see how beautiful my body is after the hail storm of distaste for the size of my waist, my skin's uneven colors, texture, shape. Luckily the moon and stars paint the sky each night, they'll soon give me sight, so I can see past what these words have done to me.

Words laced with scrutiny
can puncture your security
hold your confidence hostage
beneath the skin.
So be kind to yourself,
for every inch of you is wealth.

I want to read other women's stories. I am not talking about the ones they write and recite. I want to read the stories their skin screams out, the plot lines living in the fine lines, the story arcs in the stretch marks. I want to read the anecdotes thriving in the wrinkles, those dark spots, that scar, those dimples. Our skin holds a story we worry the world will think is shameful. But stories are written to be heard not hidden, fixed, or blurred, so uncensor your skin even if its conflicts inflict discomfort because we are not here to ease and appease, we are here to honor the bodies that make our life and everyone else's possible.

You feel entitled to my legs, my arms, my thighs
until we lock eyes and you realize
that even though my skin is on display
kissing the air you breathe
that does not authorize your access
to what is underneath.

The camera needed to be high, higher, the highest
like the angles we learned about in math class
from up there
my waist looks thinner
shoulders slimmer
my face occupies
most of the space
so if you happen to see
this photo of me
I won't have anxiety
about whether my body
embodies your idea of beauty

He said, "I want to see you naked"
so I peeled the clothes off my heart and mind.

SOUL

Narratives we are fed as girls become twine
wrapped around every thought we have.
May these words be the scissors
sharp enough to cut it all up
leave the twine behind
release every thought
while the narratives rot.

These values, their cores
have left me with sores
so sour and tender
it feels as if I'll be undoing them forever.
But I'd rather spend forever unraveling
than to live untrue
for me
for her
for you.

"Make me a sandwich, would ya?"
Darling, the only kitchen I desire to be imprisoned by
is one littered with pens, pencils, and empty notebooks
begging for the sticky, sweet meals this brain cooks.

Constantly pacifying ourselves, putting our opinions and feelings on shelves, out of reach so as not to breach the unspoken contract that holds women responsible for everyone's feelings, for mending, rebuilding, for healing. But we are tired of policing our words, sugarcoating our verbs for your comfort, so instead of playing small by constantly repenting and misrepresenting what we truly mean, we are reserving "I'm sorry" for more deserving scenes.

She allowed her emotions to take over her
and many tried to stop her from doing so
to save her from herself.
She allowed her thoughts to wander erratically
and many tried to fix the disorganization
to help her find herself.
But she didn't need to be saved or found
she needed space to water the wildflowers in her mind
to plant her feet in her own garden beneath the ground.

Being called hot, pretty, or sexy is nice but have you ever been told you light up a room when you aren't even in it or that your energy shifts the air other people breathe or that flowers bloom brighter when you walk by or that your mind is such a gift it's wrapped in a million layers of gold paper or that the mere thought of you can both start and settle a storm.

Samantha
Age: 35
Gender: female
Interested in: my peace
Location: home

Dating Profile Summary

I am my own home. It is peaceful here. Will you amplify my peace or disrupt it? If the answer is anything but amplify, boy bye.

I want to apologize to all the women I ever treated as competition. All for the male gaze, a wonder that never stays, it simply strays from one to another, the next, the other. My younger self was unaware, oblivious to the brilliance that lived in sisterhood. I never made good on our potential for powerful connection. Instead, I spread a collection of comments degrading you to feed the few fleeting butterflies he put inside.

I wish I could go back. I'd copy and paste this version of me in place of that girl that made it seem like the attention of men mattered more than the many doors we could have opened for each other. I cannot go back, but I can link arms with you here and now, lay the vying to rest so the only thing we ever contest is repeating such divisiveness for the attention of undeserving men.

I'd tell you to put the mirrors down and just feel yourself, learn to love your body without them, but doing so would rob you of marveling in the absolute vision that you are.

So do both.

There is nothing shameful about how our bodies curve
how our hips shift and dip in different seasons
how we bleed in order to plant seeds
these bodies of ours are made of the sun
of the stars
they bring light
make life.

Shame has no place here.

Him: "What is your favorite feature about yourself?"

Me: "My soul, my brain, my unique ability to strain
        Pain itself."

Him: "Well, I love your legs, your lips, the way your
        Hips are dipped in sugar."

Me: "Yes, my body is a work of art. How telling of
        your intention that that is where you chose
        to start."

So you've fallen in love with a brave woman?
Your comfort zone must be chaos and ferocity.
Your choice of flower for her must be wild plucked
from its root with your very hands drenched is truth.

Her love is warmer than average
because the rays of the sun run through her veins.
This is also why she burns those who cut her.

Women before me cracked open the sky
so the world could feel their anguish.
I will not let your cloudy thoughts eclipse
the sunshine and storms they poured into me.

Our bodies are delicate ecosystems
they bleed, shed, they spread
they create and feed
everyone needs
these bodies
to have life.
Such divinity should never
be met with indignity
we only accept affinity.

Some men treat us
like they have forgotten
they are half-woman.
Made from our very bones.

I was made to think femininity was fraught with frailty
so I favored masculinity but failed to see
we harbor a balanced beauty
a spectrum of grace, strength, and poise
everything that deploys the good in people.

My body is a song in my mother's name.
I will no longer turn its volume down
so it feels soft on your ears.

She isn't just yours.
She is a field of flowers
a landscape of love
an ocean of storms.
She is an entire universe.

"Stay humble."
Stay true,
claim your space
claim your time
claim your trophy.

Don't tell me you thought
it was simply a place
to put a piece of yourself inside
when this is where magic resides.

— we are portals

I never realized my mouth carried beauty
because I always kept it closed.
When I finally dared to open it
a garden blossomed on my tongue.

Wildflowers grow in every and any color
they sprout, stray, poke every which way
eccentric, erratic, emotional
when cut, they return
unapologetically reborn
and while some will see them as weeds
invasive debris
they forever declare:
"My value does not depend on you understanding me"

It is wild to think the woman I am becoming
is a product of the woman I was
only because
I decided to be unwavering
in unlearning it all
and returning to myself.

We are carved out of the earth
in the image
of women
who sacrificed
women of all colors
all walks of life
women rife
with fire
so I will live loudly
devoutly
for them.

She is powerful not because she is fearless. She has many fears. She is powerful because she can see herself on the other side of those fears.

The cost of getting every man to like me was me not liking myself, was me dimming the very womanhood that made me magic, that lit spaces up and made seats for other women to erupt into the world and paint it bold.

We are fire.
And while it is
warm and welcoming
it is also fierce
burning
brandish.

When you call us beautiful
I hope you mean its true definition.
An undisputable vision
not just pleasing to the eyes
one with the audacity of the sunrise.
Women are not simply aesthetic beings to gaze upon
we are creatures the mind fawns
souls that serenade the senses.
So when you call us beautiful, I hope you do not mean
the petty, predictable version of pretty.

Younger me morphed when passing by boys.
Straight steps to gliding hips.
I'd ditch my authenticity for duplicity
and put on quite a show.
Their gaze, the ultimate validation.
Their scoff, damnation.
What power I gave them.
They determined whether my value grew
or was cut at the stem.
Sometimes I still change the way I walk
they mutter some locker room talk.
The difference?
I avow, their reaction holds no weight now.
It is for my entertainment
an arraignment, if you will.

A man once said to me, "The higher your skirt, the lower your standards." As if his words would control my narrative or shift my plot, as if he was the main character.

I reminded him that my story will not be coauthored.

When the world asked:
"Will he think you are beautiful? Will he like it?"
You asked: "Do you feel beautiful? Do you like it?"
Unknowingly, my first blind date became
my first lesson in feminism.
A lesson in loving myself first.
Thanks mom.

I remember thinking the purpose of life was to *find* myself
as if one day my feet would be planted and I would be found
so I created elaborate maps with checkpoints, directions
a collection of stops to get me there
but after years of unlocking levels, staying the course
of course my feet still aren't planted, I am not found
I haven't landed.
It's because I had it all wrong.
It's not about *finding* ourselves
life is a far more beautiful song.
I say we burn the maps and ignore the spread
start creating ourselves instead
and shock everyone
as if they had misread
as if they had been misled.

Our peaks are high,
we don't settle our standards.
Our valleys low
so others can enter the climb.
Our caverns are wide and deep
to hold those tired from the crawl.

— we are mountains

The world will push you to accept the untrue
to see other women as rivals.
But it is futile to think we are in competition
when together, our highest selves come to fruition.
When I felt small, it was women who lifted my spirit
"I could never..." they wouldn't hear it.
When depression swallowed me whole
it was women who soothed my soul.
And whenever I leap into things unknown, things bold
this community of sages keeps hold.
So when the world pushes you to accept this narrative
that we are opponents or foes
call your women
burn that shit
and, together, marvel in the glow.

Men have said to me:
"You really are a piece of work."
Yes, I am.
I am a masterpiece.
An absolute work of art.
Filled with generations of broken beauty
A mess of experiences, learnings, and teachings
A paragon of plights survived
A wonder of the most divine
So, yes.
I am.
I am a piece of work.

"Men like women that can cook and clean."
"Cooking and cleaning is something all adults need to do for themselves."

— domestication has no gender

There was a time I feared my own voice
so I hushed it, allowed people to
talk over it
walk on it
crush it
Allowed them to stomp it down to average
so its power fell victim to their limits
it's potential invisible, non-existent.
Now the only thing I allow
is my own voice's level of loud.

Where does this table exist that everyone wants to be at?

I want a seat at the table.
I do this so women will have a seat at the table

I imagine if women do not have chairs
then its purpose is not ours, it's theirs
and so a simple seat would reek of defeat.
I have no desire to sit at those tables
that enable their control.
I brought wood, whiskey, nails.
I brought a tribe of women in torn veils.
I brought varnish to tarnish the surface with our newness.
We'll build our own table, as Jane did.
A space for the displaced
A surface for those they labeled worthless
A sprawling expanse of opportunity, of chance.
So when they look upon it, their eyes will burn
caught in the vibrating, cycle-breaking work being done.
It's our turn.

Women are medicine.

I can love myself and her.
I can love myself and him.
I can love myself and them.
Just because we are in love with who we've become
doesn't mean we have to succumb
to the selfish idea that love is linear.
On the contrary, it carries dimension.
After all, the love for myself is an extension
of everyone, everything I've mentioned.

I am not good enough for him.
But really he was just taught that
succumbing to
love, feelings, fawning
would be an unmanly dawning.
I was magic the whole time.

Don't call women aggressive, instead call them ambitious.
Don't call women bossy, instead call them assertive.
Oh but a rose by any other name would not smell as sweet.
I am aggressive. I am bossy.
The words are only slander
when we give them power.
Dismantle their pandor.
No more correcting,
redirecting or letting
their words curve our nerves.
Just blank stares that suddenly make
the air they breathe thick.
Their intention is weak.
What I call myself reigns king.
"so aggressive" "so bossy"
What, like it's a bad thing?

I have no desire to be like them, to be like men.
We are different on purpose.
Each drawn to life, rife with radiance.
But the world steals ours to empower their dominance.
I do not wish to be like them, to be like men.
I only wish to exist as I am
free of conditions, partitions
that keep me small
while they are big,
consuming us all.

Younger me asked, "Who are you?"
I responded, "mother, daughter, sister, friend, partner."
She smiled and said, "Those are things you are for other people. I asked who you are?"

And when you get to that point
when the sun has replaced your heart
and the moon has replaced your mind
and the ocean has replaced the moisture in your mouth
and the butterflies other people used to make you feel
are now put there by you and you alone
when you get to that point
you will scare people
because you will only ever
love out of want not need
because you will be whole
all on your own.

They hate that we feel everything all at once.
That we cry when we see others suffer
even though we don't know them
and we will never meet them.
That we sit in solitude for hours
feeling the weight of something.
They hate it because they think
all these feelings make us weak
but they are simply unaware of our sequence.

First, we feel.
Then, we heal.
And finally, we reach for our matches.

When we see stars, we aren't actually looking at them.
We are looking at the light that comes from them
after they collapse at the hands of gravity.
It takes years for the light to grace our eyes
so much so, that the original vessel
the original version of the star
that once held the light inside
doesn't exist anymore.

A star destroys itself to release the most radiant vision
our eyes will ever know.

You are a star.

I had to love myself slowly
re-read my own pages
and be patient with the parts I didn't like.
I had to trade my matches and ashes
for love, laughter, water.
Otherwise, I was never going to grow.

The woman I was meant to be always lived within me.
I wish she had bloomed sooner
so she could have lived stronger, lighter, longer.
I guess that's why I was blessed with a daughter.

WILD

I put on your coat to protect you from the cold
I put on your seatbelt to protect you in the car
I put on your helmet to protect you on a bike
I pack your bag with everything to protect you from
unpreparedness, scrapes, hunger, bug bites.

But what of the emotional turmoil?
From the narratives rooted in my own soil?
How do I protect you from the ills of the world?
From how it tries to tame girls?

The only way I know is with words.
Raw, transparent
words that curve
that swerve.
Words that seep into your heart
so deep they sweep any sound that subdues.
Words that climb into your soul
create a home so familiar, so warm
they'll warn you
when others tote fear.

Yes, I will fill you with herds upon herds
of unfiltered words
those will be your weapons
your protection.

The world will have hopes for you
and it will be impatient as you grow.
It will hope you are beautiful
you are polite
you are "good"
(whatever that means)
Oh yes, the world cannot wait
to see you become a woman
decorated with its hopes.

Me?

I cannot wait to see you serve this world
the finest cup of your love and your fury.

"Peter Peter Pumpkin eater,
Had a wife but couldn't keep her;
He was raised a feminist, it's true
So he understood just what to do;
He let her go, for she said "no"
And they both started their lives anew."

"There was an old woman who lived in a shoe
Had so many children and did the best she could do
She gave them some broth without any bread
She rocked them all soundly and put them to bed.
They woke the next day, bellies full and hearts aglow
Her best, it's true, made their love grow."

"What are little boys made of?
What are little boys made of?
Snips and snails,
And puppy-dogs' tails.
Sugar and spice,
And everything nice.
That's what little boys are made of!

What are little girls made of?
What are little girls made of?
Snips and snails,
And puppy-dogs' tails.
Sugar and spice,
And everything nice.
That's what little girls are made of!"

— your upgraded nursery rhymes

To the young girls that feel it all:
I know you are exhausted
I sense your energy for miles
don't be quick to wipe your tears
to smile
sit in your rain
let it soak you
there are other seasons
beautiful ones
where the rain will
speak in blissful tongues.
I promise.

When you read my words, my hope is not that you look for my meaning. No. My hope is that you find your own.

The ego lives behind the narratives, feeds them, greets them, needs them to exist. But the echo? The echo creates and reverberates. It doesn't see others' successes as a burden, oh no it invites those women, lifts their voices, fights for their choices. To be an echo is to never let go of the reason we exist, and I believe it is this: to share a diverse series of sounds that reflect you, me, her, the next. Sounds that vibrate the ground and show young girls we wear nothing but crowns. Sounds that don't other, rather they loudly serve one another.

We will fill the air with fluencies, feelings, flows.
We will be echoes.

all the words women have been forced to swallow
they do not drift or fade, leaving us hollow
they live in our every fiber, a fire
waiting to be coughed up, called upon
redrawn for a grand movement
meant to manifest
a path paved in pearls
for the little boys and girls
that walk behind us
all our sunken words
they will return
they will be the sweetest hymns
passed down to them
so no one, ever again
will be forced to swallow
letters meant to make the world less hollow

May you be so powerful the sky holds tension for you.
May you be so kind that the sun bows to your heart.
May you be so intuitive the wind listens for your words.
May you be so brave the ocean carries hope on your behalf.

Destroy the part of you that believes you are anything less than a bouquet of wildflowers picked from the rarest garden, anything less than magic.

cleanse it of competition
strip it of sexualization
rid it of ridicule
free it from fragility
untame its identity
allow its awkwardness
wield its wildness
embrace its everything

protect girlhood
it will be what changes us
what saves us

These words are not just mine.
They are my mothers
her mother's, and the mothers before them.
These words are water spanning generations
finally flowing freely through me.
And, someday, they will reach the shores of our daughters.
We hope they never carry them back out to sea.
We hope they scatter them in the skies,
set them free.

~~A career~~
~~A man~~
~~A child~~
~~the end.~~
    — paint your own portrait of fulfillment

Soak your words in tenderness before showering your body with them, and marvel in the garden that grows on your skin.

Don't tell girls to smile.
Instead, tell them to dream.

It feels like conceit at first
for modesty is centuries-old
and we are meant to behold
rather than be bold.
But I promise you
loving yourself is not vanity
it is sanity
it is not egoism
it's heroism.
Modesty conditioned us
a condition robbing us of joy
of love
of lust
for everything we are.

You are gentle and strong
You are soft and fiery
You are wild and steady
You are firm with love
drenched in hope
radiating light.
You contain multitudes.

The world will tell you your body is not yours.
Don't listen.
It will tell you what it should and should not endure.
Don't listen.
When you use it how you want, it will tell you you're wrong.
Don't listen.
Embrace what you wish,
and let the world fall to its knees and fawn.

She is both sundew and sunflower.
What grows depends on how you water her.

Other people can fill your cup
but there will always be space at the top.
It will never be quite full
until you decide to fill it yourself.
When you do, an overflow so vast, so wide
riddled with the divine
will pour out.
Embrace it.
Let it grow, let it swell
let it overwhelm and yell.
Because that overflow?
That wildness?
That's you.

Know and love yourself so deeply that everyone
who crosses your path will be in competition
with your peace, with your solitude.
It is then that you will know the difference
between love and control
between someone offering their heart
versus manipulating yours
between someone who amplifies you
versus molds you into a smaller version of yourself.

There are people who will try to set our words on fire so they don't have to face the truth that lives in every letter. They burn them and use what smolders to keep their own thoughts warm. But dare I warn, they have one thing right: our words are flammable, so be careful with your matches.

When you stare in the mirror
you pick, poke, stick
every insult on your skin.
My beauty, you do not understand
the light you cast
the glow that flows
from your every pore
your soul.

When you create the version of yourself
you've always dreamed, speak softly.
She and the women before her
have carried loud voices long enough.

To those that will love our daughters:

She is being raised to love out of want, not need.
To swallow this world up
and dance to her own design.
To love herself first
and swim to every corner of her dreams.
To sear her voice into the skies
and run amongst the rain.
To worship her imperfections
and shower herself with affirmation.
To nourish every inch of her soul
and fill the empty spaces with warmth.
To marvel at her own magic
and use it to light up the world.
So love her
but leave her wild.

ABOUT THE AUTHOR

Hi. I am Samantha, poet, blogger, and mother to Zuri. I believe writing is about tasting life, unearthing one's purpose, evoking change, and staying connected to ourselves and one another in an otherwise disconnected world.

I am happy you are here.
www.samanthalazo.com

Made in the USA
Monee, IL
23 November 2024

70835356R00096